CIPS STUDY M/

PROFESSIONAL DI
PROCUREMENT AND SUPPLY

REVISION NOTES

Legal aspects in procurement and supply (UK)

© Profex Publishing Limited, 2012

Printed and distributed by:
The Chartered Institute of Purchasing & Supply, Easton House, Easton on the Hill, Stamford, Lincolnshire PE9 3NZ
Tel: +44 (0) 1780 756 777
Fax: +44 (0) 1780 751 610
Email: info@cips.org
Website: www.cips.org

First edition December 2012

Contents

Page

Preface

Welcome to your Revision Notes.

Your Revision Notes are a summarised version of the material contained in your Course Book. If you find that the Revision Notes refer to material that you do not recollect clearly, you should refer back to the Course Book to refresh your memory.

There is space at the end of each chapter in your Revision Notes where you can enter your own notes for reference.

A note on style

Throughout your Study Packs you will find that we use the masculine form of personal pronouns. This convention is adopted purely for the sake of stylistic convenience – we just don't like saying 'he/she' all the time. Please don't think this reflects any kind of bias or prejudice.

December 2012

CHAPTER 1

Overview of English Law

The exam syllabus

Relevance to procurement and supply:

- Requirements are constantly changing
- Compliance is required and enforced by various sanctions and penalties
- The common law principle that 'ignorance of the law is no excuse'
- Procurement and supply involve a number of activities which are the specific focus of law and regulation – notably, the development and performance of contracts with suppliers
- If you know how complex the law is, you will seek professional advice when necessary!

The meaning of law

English legal system incorporates the law of England and Wales. Scotland and Northern Ireland have different legal systems.

Civil law assists individuals to recover property or enforce obligations owed to them.

Criminal law is designed to suppress crime, and is largely enforced by the state.

Civil cases are usually referred to in the form *Smith v Jones (1999):* the first named person (Smith) is the claimant, and the second individual is the defendant.

The sources of law

English law derives from four main sources.

- **Common law:** basis of fundamental legal principles, based on *judicial precedent*
- **Equity**: discretionary rules and remedies devised by courts on the basis of fairness (supersedes common law where there is a conflict)
- **Statute law:** Acts of Parliament and delegated legislation (statutory instruments), binding on everyone in the jurisdiction (supersedes common law and equity)
- **European Community (EC) law:** regulations, directives and decisions, based on treaties, which are enacted into statute by member states.

The doctrine of judicial precedent

If the facts of a previous case are similar to the present situation, in most circumstances the decision of the first court should be binding on the later court.

- **Ratio decidendi** – legal reasoning behind the decision
- **Obiter dictum** – statements or judgements not directly related to the case at hand: not binding on future judges
- **Stare decisis** – 'stand by a decision': judges decide cases in accordance with precedents.

The hierarchy of the Courts

Ratio decidendi must be applied in any similar case heard in a court which is on the same level, or below the level in the hierarchy, of the court originally making the decision.

Hierarchy of civil courts (highest to lowest):

- European Court of Justice (appellate court)
- House of Lords (appellate court)
- Court of Appeal
- High Court
- Divisional Courts (Chancery, Family, Queen's Bench incl. Commercial)
- Crown Courts, County Courts, Magistrates' Courts (domestic), Tribunals

The nature of precedent

A precedent will not be binding if:

- It has been overruled by a higher court
- It has been overruled by statute
- It was made per incuriam (through lack of care)
- The facts of the earlier case are materially different
- The ratio decidendi cannot be clearly followed.

OWN NOTES

OWN NOTES

CHAPTER 2

Contracts and Contract Terms

The nature of a contract

Contract: agreement between two or more parties which is *intended to be enforceable by the law*. Agreement between commercial enterprises: *presumed* intention to enforce.

Role of a contract is to set out the roles, rights and obligations of both parties in a transaction or relationship.

Outline of contract law

Four basic questions:

*   Is there a contract in existence?
*   Is the agreement one which the law should recognise and enforce?
*   When and how do the obligations of the parties come to an end?
*   What remedies are available if either party is in breach of its contractual obligations?

General principles relating to contracts

Freedom of contract: parties are at liberty to make their own bargain, and the courts will not interfere with the terms they agree upon. *Exceptions:* standard terms; implied terms; 'unfair' terms under Unfair Contract Terms Act 1977 (eg exclusion clauses)

Sanctity of contract: agreement cannot be interfered with by the parties, courts, or third parties. Parties to a contract must abide by it unless released from obligations by the other party. *Exceptions:* agreements 'frustrated' by circumstances beyond control.

Bilateral and unilateral contracts

Bilateral contract: both parties make promises and are bound (eg sale of goods).

Unilateral contract: one party (the promisor) makes a promise and is bound, while other person (promisee) is free to perform or not. *Carlill v Carbolic Smokeball Co (1893):* promisor is bound to reward promise, if promisee performs the act which the promisor promised to reward.

Essential elements in a binding contract

- **Agreement:** exchange of **offer** and **acceptance**. Offeror must make a definite promise to be bound on specific terms. Offeree must accept the offer, clearly, unconditionally and freely (ie not subject to duress or undue influence).
- **Consideration**: each party must suffer some kind of loss or 'detriment' in return for benefit received.
- **Intention** to create legal relations
- **Contractual capacity**: each of the parties must be legally able to enter into a contract.
- **Correct form**: the contract must be in a valid form (not necessarily in writing), with particular requirements for certain types of agreement.

Terms and representations

A statement made during negotiations leading to a contract, may be:

- A **term** of the subsequent contract, defining the content of the agreement *or merely*
- A **representation** designed to 'induce' the contract.

Why important? If a *representation* is found to be untrue: remedies for misrepresentation. If a *term* is found to be untrue: remedies for breach of contract + misrepresentation.

Intention of the parties

Whether a statement becomes a term depends on the intention of the parties, determined by: when statement made; whether in writing; how important *[Bannerman v White, 1861]*; whether suggested other party check accuracy or not *[Schawel v Reade, 1913]*; and whether person making statement has special knowledge *[Dick Bentley Productions Ltd v Harold Smith (Motors) Ltd, 1965]* or not *[Oscar Chess Ltd. v Williams, 1957]*

Express and implied terms

Terms must be complete and certain of meaning *[King's Motors (Oxford) Ltd v Lax, 1969]*

Express terms: explicitly inserted into contract by parties: by negotiation, 'standard' terms of business or 'model' form contract. Eg exclusion clause or *force majeure*

Implied terms: automatically assumed to be part of a contract by virtue of:

- Statute: eg SGA 1979, implied term of satisfactory quality and fitness for purpose
- Custom of trade or locality
- Nature of contract: eg landlord's duty of care *[Liverpool City Council v Irwin, 1977]*
- Business efficacy (workability of agreement) *[Eg The Moorcock, 1889]*

Interpretation of contract terms

If there is ambiguity in a contractual term, courts:

- Favour an interpretation that will give effect to the contract (vs voiding it)
- Interpret against the person seeking to rely on it for benefit (***contra proferentem rule***).

Conditions and warranties

Conditions are vital terms of contract: breach entitles wronged party to 'repudiate' (cancel) the contract + damages for losses suffered *[Poussard v Spiers, 1876]*

Warranties are non-vital terms of contract: breach only entitles wronged party to damages: mutual obligations remain in place *[Bettini v Gye, 1876]*

Innominate (intermediate) terms: may be treated as a condition or warranty *depending* on the effect of breach *[Hong Kong Fir Shipping Co v Kawasaki, 1962]*

The implications of international law

The Vienna Convention on the International Sales of Goods

Uniform Law on Sales

- The seller has three fundamental duties: to deliver the goods, to deliver the relevant documentation; and to transfer the property in the goods
- The buyer has two duties: to pay the price expressed in the contract of sale, and to take delivery of goods according to the terms of the contract of sale.

Uniform Law on Formation

- An offer can be revoked *unless* it states a fixed time for acceptance, or if it specifically states that it is irrevocable, or if revocation is not made in good faith.
- Qualified acceptance (other than very minor qualification) is a counter-offer.

Applicable law and jurisdiction

Rome Convention + UK Contracts (Applicable Law) Act 1990: determines the law that applies to a contract, where there is choice between the laws of different countries.

Parties may agree on which law will be applicable by express clause.

If not expressed, applicable law may be inferred from nature of contract and circumstances: law with which the contact is most closely associated.

OWN NOTES

CHAPTER 3

Offer and Acceptance

The essence of contract law is to ensure that the parties to a contract are basically in agreement. 'Consensus ad idem': 'mutual assent' or 'meeting of the minds'.

The offer

Requirements for valid offer

- Clear, definite, unequivocal statement of willingness to be bound in contract
- Including all terms of the proposed contract (expressly or by implication)
- Made to person, class of persons or whole world [Carlill v Carbolic Smokeball Co, 1893]
- Clearly communicated to offeree [R v Clarke, 1927; Tinn v Hoffman, 1873: cross-offers]
- Must be 'open' (still in force) when accepted.

Termination of the offer

Revocation (cancellation or annulment) by offeror:

- At any time prior to acceptance [Errington v Errington, 1953] – even if offer is open 'for a stated time' [Routledge v Grant]
- Expressly or by implication [Dickinson v Dodds, 1876]
- Communicated by offeror or reliable third party [Dickinson v Dodds, 1876]
- Taking effect only when received/understood [Byrne v Van Tienhoven, 1880]

Rejection: outright (stated non-acceptance) or by counter-offer (conditional acceptance on varied terms).

- **Counter-offer** (a) closes original offer and (b) makes original offeree the offeror: [Hyde v Wrench, 1840]
- Request for further details is not a counter-offer [Stevenson v McClean, 1880]

Lapse: (a) after stated time period for expiration, (b) after a 'reasonable length of time', (c) after failure of condition to which offer was subject, (d) on death of offeror.

Situations where there is no offer

Not all statements by a buyer or supplier amount to an 'offer' – and only an offer can be accepted, leading to a contract.

Invitation to treat: not an offer, but an invitation to others to make an offer. Eg:

- Display of goods [Pharmaceutical Society of Great Britain v Boots, 1953]
- Advertisement to sell [Partridge v Crittenden, 1968]

Statement of intention (eg in advertisement): not an offer. *[Harris v Nickerson, 1873]*

Statement of price in answer to enquiry: not an offer, but a supply of information: [*Harvey v Facey, 1893]* – BUT a **quotation** could be construed as being an offer, if detailed and specific enough to be accepted simply by saying 'yes'.

Acceptance

Acceptance is an **unconditional** assent to all the terms of an offer.

Attempt by the offeree to change or qualify terms makes a counter-offer *[Hyde v Wrench]*

Form of acceptance

Any form of acceptance is valid, whether oral, written, or inferred from conduct *[Carlill; Brogden v Metropolitan Railway, 1877]*

Offeror may stipulate mandatory form of acceptance BUT:

- If only requested, any other form is valid *[Yates Building v R J Pulleyn & Sons, 1975]*
- May not stipulate that silence is acceptance *[Felthouse v Bindley, 1863]*

Communication of acceptance

Offeree has responsibility to ensure that acceptance is properly communicated.

Acceptance is complete when the offeror has received and understood acceptance, BUT:

Postal rule: acceptance complete when letter posted *[Adams v Lindsell, 1818]*, where:

- Post is the chosen, obvious or reasonable method of acceptance
- Letter is properly posted *[Re London and Northern Bank ex parte Jones, 1900]*

Tenders

A tender is an offer to supply specified goods or services at a stated cost or rate.

If an offer to work on a 'one-off' job = offer that can be accepted, completing contract.

If a 'standing offer' to supply a series of things: each acceptance (placement of order) completes a distinct contract *[Great Northern Railways v Witham, 1873]*

Buyer's obligations under a tender

Not in breach of contract if places fewer or no orders under a standing offer [*Percival v London County Council, 1918]*

In breach of contract if agrees to take all requirements from successful tenderer, but orders goods from others *[Kier v Whitehead Iron Co, 1938]*

Not required to accept lowest tender, *unless* states that it will do so in the ITT *[Harvela Investments Ltd v Royal Trust Company of Canada]*

Must give due consideration to tenders complying with ITT *[Blackpool & Fyle Aero Club Ltd v Blackpool Borough Council, 1990) –* 'collateral obligation'.

Precedence of terms

'Battle of the forms': buyer and seller standard terms of business; exchange of forms (quotation, order, acknowledgement, delivery note); cycle of 'counter-offers' *[Butler Machine Tool Co Ltd v Ex-Cell-O Corporation, 1979]*

'Last document rule': last set of terms and conditions sent (eg delivery note) constitutes the final counter-offer (accepted when buyer accepts goods).

Preventative measures: acknowledgement copies of enquiries and purchase orders (supplier sign and return, accepting buyer's terms); negotiated terms and conditions (high value contracts; check terms attached to supplier documentation; stamp delivery notes 'goods received on buyer's terms and conditions'.

If goods are transferred and used, without contract being formed: **'quasi contract'**. Buyer must pay what goods are worth (*quantum meruit).*

OWN NOTES

CHAPTER 4

Consideration

The nature of consideration

One party doing something *because* the other party is doing something, on the basis of:

- Benefit or detriment *[Currie v Misa, 1875]*
- The price of a promise *[Dunlop v Selfridge, 1915]*

Executed consideration: promise made in return for the performance of an act *[Carlill v Carbolic Smokeball Co Ltd, 1893]*

Executory consideration: exchange of promises to do something in the future.

The rules relating to consideration

Consideration must be valuable, but need not be adequate
- 'Valuable': having some monetary value *[Thomas v Thomas, 1842]*
- Need not be objectively sufficient to pay for promise received *[Chappell & Co v Nestlé Co Ltd, 1960]*

Consideration must be sufficient: 'sufficient' = something the law recognises as consideration.

Acts NOT held to constitute sufficient consideration:

- **Performance of existing duty imposed by law** *[Collins v Godefroy, 1831]*
    BUT: action *over and above* legal requirement = sufficient *[Glasbrook Brothers Ltd v Glamorgan CC, 1925]*
- **Performance of existing duty imposed by contract** *[Stilk v Myrick, 1809]*
    BUT: *new* element to requirement or promise = sufficient *[Hartley v Ponsonby, 1857; Williams v Roffey Brothers, 1990]*
- **'Past consideration':** Promise in return for an act or promise *already* performed unilaterally by the other party = not in response to each other, so no contract *[Re McArdle, 1951]*
- **Performance/promise of an illegal act.**

Consideration must move from the promisee: The person wishing to enforce contract must show that he personally provided consideration *[Tweddle v Atkinson, 1861]*

The problem of part-payment

Rule in *Pinnel's case (1602)*: payment of a lesser sum cannot be satisfaction for the whole sum [also *Foakes v Beer, 1884*].

Even if the creditor has promised to accept lesser sum, no 'sufficient consideration' has been given: legal action can still be taken to recover whole sum. [NB only in undisputed, liquidated (fixed value) claims.]

BUT this may lead to unfairness, if creditor goes back on promise to accept lesser sum. Provisions for part payment:

- **Variation of terms at the creditor's request:** 'accord' (agreement to accept less) and 'satisfaction' (new element introduced at creditor's request, as consideration for not claiming the balance [*D & C Builders v Rees, 1966]:* eg earlier payment.
- **Part-payment by a third party:** if creditor agrees to accept part-payment from a third party, he can't also claim balance from debtor *[Hirachand Punamchand v Temple, 1911]*
- **Composition with creditors:** where party is unable to pay debts, and all creditors agree to accept part-payment in full satisfaction of claims. (Consideration = promise of each creditor not to claim full debt, so that no one creditor benefits at expense of others.)
- **Equitable concept of promissory estoppel** (see below)

The doctrine of promissory estoppel

Equitable concept of **promissory estoppel** may operate to prevent a creditor going back on an unequivocal promise to accept a lesser amount.

Central London Property Trust Ltd v High Trees House Ltd (1947): promise not to claim the full amount was 'intended to be acted upon, and in fact acted upon', making it binding.

BUT:

- 'A shield not a sword': intended to be used by defendant (against claim to recover full amount)
- May have only 'suspensory' effect: waived arrears are irrecoverable, but future payments may be demanded in full.

OWN NOTES

OWN NOTES

CHAPTER 5

Intention, Capacity and Form

Intention to create legal relations

Domestic and social arrangements: presumption of no intention for agreement to be legally binding *[Balfour v Balfour, 1919]* – but court may decide otherwise, if formal financial arrangements made *[Parker v Clark, 1960]*.

Commercial agreements: strong presumption of intention to be legally binding – unless agreement expresses contrary intention eg 'binding in honour only' *[Jones v Vernon's Pools Ltd, 1938]*

Collective agreements (eg made by trade unions and employers' associations): presumption of no intention to be legally binding – unless expresses contrary intention.

Letters of intent (designed to commence work while final terms are negotiated): no binding contract exists. Only reasonable price (*quantum meruit*) can be claimed for work performed *[British Steel Corporation v Cleveland Bridge & Engineering Co Ltd, 1984]*.

Capacity to contract

Persons have capacity to contract on their own behalf *except:* minors, the mentally disordered and those under the influence of drugs or alcohol.

Corporations are recognised legal persons with capacity to contract, *but NOT:*

- Prior to incorporation *[Kelner v Baxter, 1866]*
- *Ultra vires* (pre-2006): outside the stated 'objects' of the corporation (not applied to 'companies' registered under the Companies Acts)

Persons on behalf of corporations:

- Absolute capacity: owner, partners or directors; agents with formally delegated powers to act on the company's behalf.
- If agent acts in excess of actual authority, principal will still be bound if he has acted within his 'apparent' authority.

Form of contract

Oral contracts

Oral agreements are binding. However, preferable to put commercial agreements in writing, to minimise the risk of:

- Inability to check and confirm draft agreement in detail
- Voiding of contract due to mistake or ambiguity of terms
- Misunderstandings and contractual disputes
- Lack of transparency and audit trail

Specialty contracts

Must be made in writing: eg bills of exchange, consumer credit agreements, transfers of shares in registered companies, assignment of debts

Must be 'evidenced' in writing: contracts of guarantee

Must be in form of deed (written, signed and witnessed): eg conveyance of land, assignment of long lease

Electronic communications may be used (Electronic Communications Act 2000)

Electronic contracting

Electronic Communications Act 2000: recognises digital signatures as legally valid.

Electronic Commerce (EC Directive) Regulations 2002:

- Regulation 6: information that must appear on company emails and website; information where goods or services are provided (price + tax/delivery costs)
- Regulation 7: rules on commercial communications (must be clearly identifiable)
- Regulation 8: duty on sellers to check opt-out email registers
- Regulation 9: information to be provided for web orders.
- Regulation 11: receipts to be issued for orders placed via a website
- Regulations 13–15: if no means provided for buyer to correct input errors, buyer shall have the right to rescind the contract.

OWN NOTES

OWN NOTES

CHAPTER 6

Void and Unenforceable Contracts

Duress and undue influence

Contracts made under duress or undue influence are **voidable** by wronged party.

Duress

Where contract entered into as a result of:

- Violence *[Barton v Armstrong, 1976]* or threat of violence *[Williams v Bayley, 1866]*
- Economic duress: threat against person's goods *[Atlas Express v Kafco, 1989; Tankships v ITWF, 1983]*.

Illegitimate economic duress – vs legitimate 'hard bargaining' – where: contract is vital to defendant's business; threat of withdrawal of business is clear; no consideration given for revised terms; protest and intention to repudiate contract made clear at time pressure applied *[North Ocean Shipping v Hyundai Construction, 1978]*

Undue influence

Where party enters into a transaction under influence presenting him from freely and independently deciding upon its advisability *[Re Craig, 1971]*

- No fiduciary relationship: undue influence must be proved. Complainant may rescind (set aside) the transaction.
- Fiduciary relationship (eg solicitor and client): undue influence *presumed* to exist. Complainant can only rescind the transaction if it is manifestly disadvantageous to him.

Misrepresentation

False statement of material fact made before or at the time of entering into a contract, which was intended to (and did) induce the other party to make the contract.

A statement: express or implied by conduct. Silence is not misrepresentation *except:*

- In contracts *uberrimae fidei*: vital information must be communicated
- Where it distorts a positive representation *[Nottingham Patent Brick v Butler, 1886]*
- Where a true statement *becomes* false before contract *[With v O'Flanagan, 1936]*

Of fact: does not include statement of law; honest opinion *[Bisset v Wilkinson, 1927]*; honest intention *[Edgington v Fitzmaurice, 1885]*; or tradesman's praise of his wares.

Which is false: including true but misleading in context *[Nottingham Patent Brick v Butler]*

Made by one contracting party (or agent): if indirect, actionable only if misrepresentor intended statement to reach the misrepresentee.

Which induced the contract:

- Made prior to contract; misrepresentee aware of it *[Horsfall v Thomas, 1862]*
- Misrepresentee didn't know statement false; relied upon it *[Attwood v Small, 1838]*
- Misrepresentation need not be sole inducement *[Edgington v Fitzmaurice, 1885]*

Types of misrepresentation

Fraudulent misrepresentation: person making the statement did not honestly believe it to be true (vs merely 'inaccurate' but honestly believed: *Derry v Peek (1889)*. *Remedies:* rescission *or* damages (for tort of deceit).

Negligent misrepresentation: party making misrepresentation has a duty of care (eg in position of trust), but fails to take reasonable care (eg fails to check facts). *Remedies:* rescission (injured party may elect to affirm) *or* damages in lieu of rescission (under Misrepresentation Act 1967) *or* damages (for tort of negligence).

Innocent misrepresentation: representer has reasonable grounds for statement (though in fact untrue). *Remedies:* rescission (injured party may elect to affirm) *or* **damages in lieu of** rescission (Misrepresentation Act).

The equitable remedy of rescission

'Rescission': an equitable remedy (where a contract is voidable): sets contract aside, returning both parties to their exact pre-contract position.

Right to rescind is **lost** where: the injured party affirms the contract; there is a lapse of time; restitution is impossible; a third party's rights would be prejudiced by rescission.

Mistake

Parties end up bound by a contract to which they did not intend to commit themselves.

Parties are, in principle, bound by agreed terms *[Leaf v International Galleries, 1950; Tamplin v James, 1880]*. BUT **operative mistake:** so fundamental as to destroy intention to be bound: nullifies consent; contract *void* (no legal effect; unenforceable).

Where goods resold to innocent third party:

- If contract **void** for mistake: seller had no title, no right to sell (*nemo dat rule*)
- If contract **voidable** (discretionary), title passes *until* rescinded: resale valid.

Types of mistake

Common mistake: both parties make the same mistake. Agreement exists: may be operative (eg if goods do not exist: *Couturier v Hastie, 1852]* or not (eg re quality of goods *Bell v Lever Bros, 1932]*

Mutual mistake: parties believe they've agreed, but are at cross purposes. Contract binding where no misrepresentation or ambiguity *[Raffles v Wichelhaus, 1864]*. Correct interpretation construed from conduct of parties.

Unilateral mistake: one party is mistaken and the other is aware of this *[Webster v Cecil, 1861]*. Mistake negates consent: contract void

Mistake as to nature or effect of signed document. A person is bound by signature, unless he can plead *non est facturm* (signature obtained by trick to a fundamentally different document than intended) *[Lewis v Clay, 1897; Gallie v Lee]*

Mistake in written agreement. Court may grant order of rectification, where written document inaccurately reflects the intentions of oral agreement *[Joscelyne v Nissen, 1970]*

Void, voidable and illegal contracts

Void contract: no legal effect on either party.

Voidable contract: exists unless and until rescinded at the option of innocent party.

Unenforceable contract: valid contract, but terms cannot be enforced.

Contracts may be **illegal** (therefore void) by statute or common law: eg in restraint of trade; restricting prices (Competition Act); or inciting criminal activity.

OWN NOTES

CHAPTER 7

Discharge of Contract

Methods of discharging a contract

Performance. When a party has done what is required under the contract.

Agreement to terminate unfulfilled obligations (with sufficient consideration).

Breach: inexcusable failure by a party to a contract to fulfil some or all of his obligations under it. The other party may elect to treat the contract as being at an end.

Frustration: the contract becomes impossible to perform.

Performance

General rule: contract is discharged by performance only when both parties have complied *fully* and *exactly* with the terms of the contract *[Re Moore & Landauer, 1927]*

Entire contract: if single price agreed for performance of contract, no part of price is payable until entire contract has been exactly performed – **regardless of reasons (eg death)** *[Cutter v Powell, 1795]*.

Exceptions to ensure fairness.

- **Severable (divisible) contracts:** comprising separate obligations (eg consignments of goods). Individual contracts may be discharged separately.
- **One party prevented** from full performance by act or omission of other party. May be compensated for work completed via *quantum meruit [Planché v Colburn, 1831]* **or** damages for breach of contract.
- **Acceptance of partial performance:** if party accepts benefit of partial performance, inferred promise to pay on *quantum meruit* basis – *unless* party had no choice but to accept partial performance *[Sumpter v Hedges, 1898]*
- **Substantial performance:** if party has substantially performed duties, may recover agreed price, less damages for shortfall *[Hoenig v Isaacs, 1952]* – *unless* defects extensive *[Bolton v Mahadeva, 1972]*.
- **Conditions** must be strictly performed, but no breach of warranty justifies non-performance by the other party.

Time for performance:

- If not specified, must be 'within a reasonable time'.
- In commercial contracts, time is 'of the essence' (condition of contract) unless evidence to the contrary [*Bunge Corporation v Tradax, 1981; Hartley v Hymans, 1920*]
- In event of delay, injured party may give notice to make time of the essence [*Charles Rickards Ltd v Oppenheim, 1950*]

Agreement

Condition precedent: term of a contract preventing its taking effect *unless* a specified event occurs or act is performed (eg obtaining of licence).

Condition subsequent: term of a contract permitting discharge on happening of a specified event or act (eg giving notice).

Termination by new agreement (supported by consideration):

- Bilateral: where both parties are released from outstanding obligations
- Unilateral: where one party is released, for consideration (eg cancellation fee)
- Novation: original contract is discharged and a new one substituted.

Breach

Breach of contract occurs when:

- A party fails to perform an obligation under the contract (**actual breach**); or
- Before the time fixed to perform an obligation, a party shows an intention not to perform (**anticipatory breach**). Injured party can accept the breach (and sue immediately for breach: *Hochster v De La Tour, 1853) or* affirm the contract in hope that performance will occur.

Breach of **condition**, or substantial breach of intermediate term, or total repudiation of contract: injured party may choose to

- Treat the contract as discharged (repudiate) and claim damages for loss suffered; *or*
- Treat the contract as operative (affirm) and claim damages for any loss suffered.

Breach of warranty: injured party may claim damages only.

Frustration

General rule: party who fails to perform is liable for breach, regardless of excuse [*Paradine v Jane, 1647*]

Doctrine of frustration developed to mitigate the severity of this rule where performance becomes impossible through events beyond the control of either party.

- Destruction of subject matter [*Taylor v Caldwell, 1863*]
- Non-occurrence of event on which contract based [*Krell v Henry, 1903*]

- Incapacity (eg death), where contract requires personal performance
- Impossibility due to change in law *[Re Shipton, Anderson & Co, 1915]*
- Extensive interruption which alters performance *[Metropolitan Water Board v Dick Keer & Co Ltd, 1918]*

BUT NOT:

- Contract merely more difficult or expensive to perform *[Tsakiroglou v Noblee Thorl, 1960]*
- Party unable to achieve undertaking *[Cassidy v Osuustukkukauppa, 1957]*

Law Reform (Frustrated Contracts) Act 1943: frustrated contract automatically discharged; sums paid under contract must be repaid; sums payable cease to be payable.; benefits must be paid for. (Unless *force majeure* clause in place.)

7

OWN NOTES

CHAPTER 8

Remedies for Non-Performance

Types of remedy arising on breach of contract

Damages: financial compensation for losses suffered as a result of the breach.

Specific performance: court orders defendant to carry out obligations under contract

Injunction: court order requires or forbids a person to do something

Quantum meruit: a party is entitled to fair payment for work performed under contract

Action for the price (statutory remedy): seller may sue buyer for agreed payment.

Damages

Damages put injured party into position it would have been in if the contract had been properly performed: 'compensatory' not 'punitive'.

Unliquidated damages: contract makes no provision; court determines damages

Liquidated damages: contract expressly provides for fixed sum on breach, as genuine attempt to estimate loss *[Dunlop Pneumatic Tyre Co v New Garage, 1915]*. Injured party can *only* claim liquidated amount *[Cellulose Acetate Slik Co v Widnes Foundry]*.

Penalty clause: framed to deter breach, without genuine attempt to estimate loss. Void: injured party can sue for unliquidated damages. Construed as penalty clause if:

- Sum stipulated is excessive (not genuine attempt to pre-estimate loss)
- Single sum payable on wide range of breaches *[Kemble v Farren, 1829]*

Assessment of unliquidated damages: remoteness of damage

Remoteness of damage: what losses arise (consequential loss) from the breach?

Loss to be compensated *[Hadley v Baxendale, 1854]* should be such as may reasonably be considered either:

- To **arise naturally** from the breach of contract (general damages or normal loss) *or*
- To be **foreseeable** when contract was made as the result of breach (special damages or

abnormal loss)

- Depending on any special knowledge which parties possess *[Victoria Laundry v Newman Industries, 1949]*
- Regardless of whether the extent of damage was foreseen *[H Parson Livestock v Uttley Ingham & Co, 1978]*

Assessment of unliquidated damages: measure of damages

Measure of damages: amount which will, so far as money can, put the claimant in the position in which he would have been had the contract been performed.

If no actual loss suffered, nominal *[Surrey County Council v Bredero Homes Ltd, 1993]*

Difficulty of loss estimation no barrier *[Chaplin v Hicks, 1911]*

Claimant must take reasonable steps to mitigate loss *[Brace v Calder, 1895]*

Service credits

Pre-specified financial amounts, to which a buyer becomes entitled if agreed service levels (as defined in the contract or SLA) are not achieved.

Contract may stipulate that service credit mechanism is *not* a form of liquidated damages, but a mechanism for varying service charges according to different levels of performance. (Remedies not constrained by need to estimate losses.)

Parties may agree a 'termination threshold', based on the level of service credits accrued over a specified period, giving a right of termination in the face of persistent defaults.

Specific performance and injunction

Specific performance

Equitable remedy whereby court orders the defendant to carry out obligations under the contract. Will NOT be ordered:

- Where damages are an adequate remedy
- Where the court could not adequately supervise performance of the contract
- In a contract of personal services.

Injunction

An order of the court which either requires a person to do something (**mandatory injunction**) or prohibits a person from doing something (**prohibitory injunction**). Granted only when 'just and convenient' eg:

- Granted to restrain a party from committing a breach of contract *[Metropolitan Electric Supply v Ginder, 1901]*
- Not granted if would require specific performance, where this would be refused *[Page One Records Ltd v Britton, 1967]*

Quantum meruit

Equitable remedy where a contract has been part-performed, but where the innocent party is prevented from completing the contract by the conduct of the defaulting party.

Where there is precise provision for remuneration, *quantum meruit* cannot usually be used to alter the price, even if extra work is done *[Gilbert & Partners v Knight, 1968]*

Termination of relationship

Key issues in termination (Lysons & Farringdon): Timing; relationship; legal considerations; succession issues.

Non-contractual rights to terminate

Breach of condition, material breach of an intermediate term, or repudiation: does not automatically terminate the contract. Injured party *may* repudiate or affirm.

Breach of warranty: contract not terminated.

Anticipatory breach: injured party may accept breach (contract discharged) or affirm the contract.

Frustration: contract terminated where circumstances prevent performance as intended, with neither party in default.

Breach of contract for sale of goods: statutory remedies under SGA 1979.

Contractual provisions

Duration clause: specifying contract period, with commencement and expiry dates.

Termination for default clause: allowing termination in case of material default or breach of contract

Break provision: allowing termination 'at will' or 'for convenience'. May need to justify reasons as 'rational, honest and proper' and provide for contractor compensation on *quantum meruit* basis. May not be used to obtain better price from another contractor *[Abbey Development v PP Brickwork, 2003]*

Step-in clause: allowing outsourcer to temporarily re-assume responsibility for work, in the event of serious breach of contract or service failure.

Transition clause: stipulating co-operation of outgoing contractor during handover arising from completion or earlier termination of contract eg access to documents, return of assets.

Serving notices

Notice may be required to trigger termination of contract, as well as eg commencement of legal proceedings. Contract should expressly stipulate:

- How notice should be served (eg in writing, by email, by personal delivery)
- On whom notice should be served (where applicable)
- The period of notice which can be invoked by either party in specified circumstances.

OWN NOTES

8

OWN NOTES

CHAPTER 9

The Settlement of Commercial Disputes

Contractual disputes

OGC sequence of escalating dispute resolution techniques:

- Negotiation > Mediation > Conciliation > Adjudication > Arbitration > Litigation

Negotiated settlement

Consultation: potential causes of conflict are discussed before the problem arises

Negotiation: Purposeful Persuasion + Constructive Compromise (Gennard & Judge)

- **Distributive** approach: distribution of limited resources, or 'dividing up a fixed pie'; zero-sum game or 'win-lose' outcome.
- **Integrative** approach: collaborative problem-solving to increase the options available (or 'expanding the pie'), with the aim of exploring possibilities for both parties to find a mutually satisfying or win-win solution.

Advantages of negotiated resolution (OGC): speed; cost saving; confidentiality (with no external involvement); preservation of relationships; range of possible solutions; and control over the process and outcome.

Inadequate where: complex legal issues are involved; one party has a high degree of power; the dispute involves international contracts.

Litigation

Litigation is legal action to have a commercial or contract dispute resolved by the courts: essentially adversarial in nature.

Advantages of litigation: fair and impartial decision on merits of case; decision legally binding; threat may be sufficient to secure compliance or negotiated settlement.

Drawbacks of litigation: costly legal fees; long process (potentially disruptive to business); no confidentiality; complexity in international cases (different legal jurisdiction); adversarial approach damaging goodwill. Usually regarded as the method of 'last resort'.

Arbitration and adjudication

Arbitration

Arbitration: appointment of independent person (or panel) to consider arguments in formal, closed proceedings, and to deliver a decision, legally binding on both parties.

Arbitration agrement: disputes must be referred to arbitration before litigation *(Scott v Avery clause)*; both parties agree to be bound by the decision of arbitrator; time limits during which arbitration must begin; arbitrator must give reasons for award.

Arbitration Act 1996 (arbitration agreements): party autonomy in deciding how arbitration should be conducted; courts not allowed to intervene (except at request or in case of manifest injustice) *[Balfour Beatty v Channel Tunnel Group, 1993];* courts may support arbitral proceedings.

International frameworks: eg ICC, UNCITRAL, London Court of International Arbitration

Advantages of arbitration: privacy; less adversarial than litigation; single process (avoiding appeals); speedier and less expensive than litigation; specialist arbitrators.

Disadvantages: award may be subject to intervention by courts; arbitrators' powers less extensive than courts.

Adjudication

Process whereby expert third party, appointed by parties in a dispute, hears arguments and makes a decision. Compared to arbitration: less formal; focuses on facts of dispute (rather than points of law); less clearly binding and free from court intervention.

Dispute resolution under the Housing Grants, Construction and Regeneration Act (HGCRA).

Alternative dispute resolution

UK Civil Procedure Rules 1998: ADR is to play a central role in dispute resolution. Judges may delay a case to enable parties to go to mediation.

ADR clause: specifying ADR as mandatory first option, ADR service provider and process rules.

Conciliation: grievances are aired in negotiation, facilitated by an impartial conciliator (not 'referee' but 'dispute resolution coach'): decision reached is not legally binding (unless expressed in contract).

Mediation: appointment of independent person (or panel) who will consider the case of both sides and make a formal proposal or recommendation (not binding on either party) as a basis for settlement of the dispute.

- Eg CEDR Model Mediation Procedure and Model Mediation Agreement.
- **Mediation clause:** parties will meet in good faith effort to resolve dispute within defined period; if dispute not resolved, parties will attempt to settle by mediation; neither party may commence court proceedings or arbitration until mediation terminated or other party failed to participate in mediation.

Advantages of ADR: non-adversarial, speedy, confidential, and inexpensive; settlement designed by parties, rather than imposed; neutral third party refocuses negotiation on commercial issues.

Disadvantages of ADR: results not binding; ADR clauses may not be enforceable.

Involving lawyers

Commercial and business litigation solicitors, or dispute resolution lawyers may: advise on contract law; assess the viability of legal action; support the client through litigation; develop enforceable settlement agreements; and offer accredited commercial mediation services.

When selecting lawyers, each party should consider: their credentials and demonstrated ability in litigating similar matters; their demonstrated ability and willingness to use ADR methods.

9

OWN NOTES

CHAPTER 10

Express Terms of Contract

Sources of express terms

Negotiated agreement between the parties on specific issues of contract (complex, high-value, high-risk, non-routine contracts)

Standard contracts of purchase or supply, incorporating 'standard terms of business' (low-value, low-risk and routine purchases).

Model form contracts: published by third party experts; incorporating standard practice in contracting for specific purposes within specific industries. Eg New Engineering Contract (NEC); FIDIC construction contracts; IMechE/IEE Model Forms of General Conditions of Contract.

Standard terms of contract

General contract structure (Lysons & Farringdon):

- **General terms:** general agreements; changes, alterations and variations; notice
- **Commercial provisions:** passing of title; time of performance; inspection and testing; delivery and packing; assignment and subcontracting; liability; rejection; payment
- **Secondary commercial provisions:** confidentiality and IP; indemnity; guarantee; termination; arbitration
- **Standard clauses:** waiver; *force majeure;* law and jurisdiction.

Liability, guarantees and indemnities

Liability: legal and financial responsibility of an entity in a situation (eg for debts, damages or compensation).

- **Strict liability:** entity is legally responsible for the damage or loss caused by acts or omissions – regardless of fault (such as negligence). eg: **product liability**.
- **Vicarious liability:** superior bears responsibility for the acts of subordinate.

Guarantee (warranty) clause: supplier guarantees to make good defects in items supplied, provided that notice is received within a reasonable time.

Performance bond: sum of money set aside as a guarantee of satisfactory completion of a project by a contractor eg surety bond or Bank Guarantee (third-party 'surety' agrees to uphold contractual promises made by principal, if principal fails to meet them)

10

Contract of guarantee: contract in which one party agrees to guarantee (or stand surety for) the liability of another for debt, default or other problems (eg surety bond).

Indemnity clause: assigns primarily liability to the other party: undertaking that other party will accept liability for any claims, costs, expenses or losses incurred by the buyer as the direct or indirect result of the supplier's breach of contract obligations.

Indemnity or guarantee? [Birkmyr v Darnell, 1704]

- A and B go into a shop. B says to the shopkeeper 'Let A have the goods. If he doesn't pay you, then I will'. *Guarantee:* primary liability is with A, secondary liability with B.
- A and B go into a shop. B says to the shopkeeper 'Let A have the goods. I will see that you are paid'. *Indemnity*: B has assumed primary liability; no secondary liability.

Defects liability clause: obliges a contractor to repair or rectify defects appearing in works, during a defined 'defects liability period'.

- Sets out: the term of the defects liability period; the scope of defects; security and retention provisions; procedures for defect notification; right of contractor to remedy defects (or subcontract).
- Clause may require contractor to make good defects irrespective of cause – while agreeing to compensate the contractor for the work, where it is not in default.

Exclusion clauses

Exclusion clauses:

- Totally exclude one party from the liability which would otherwise arise from some breach of contract (such as the supply of goods of inferior quality); or
- Restrict or limit liability in some way; or
- Seek to offer some form of 'guarantee' in place of normal liability for breach of contract.

Applicability and validity of exclusion clauses

Common law test

- Clause must be **incorporated into the contract** (expressly or by custom): not added later [Olley v Marlborough Court, 1949].
- Clause must be **clear and precise** [Andrew Bros (Bournemouth) Ltd v Singer & Co Ltd, 1934]. Any ambiguity will be construed *contra proferentem* (against party seeking to rely on it: Hollier v Rambler Motors, 1972]

Statutory test (Unfair Contract Terms Act 1977):

- **Negligence** (breach of duty to take reasonable care). Person in business cannot exclude or restrict liability (a) for death or injury or (b) for loss other than death or injury unless clause is 'reasonable'.
- **Breach of contract:** any term in standard term contract or consumer contract purporting to restrict liability for breach is effective only if 'reasonable'.
- **'Reasonable'** = fair and reasonable having regard to circumstances known to parties

when contract was made *[George Mitchell (Chesterhall) Ltd v Finney Lock Seeds Ltd, 1983; Smith v Eric S Bush, 1989]*. Depends on (a) strength of bargaining positions; (b) inducements; (c) buyer awareness; (d) practicability of conditions; (e) bespoke manufacture.

Unfair Terms in Consumer Contracts Regulations 1999: 'fairness' test for consumer contracts for provision of goods or services. 'Unfair' = causes significant imbalance in parties' rights or obligations, to detriment of consumer, contrary to good faith.

Other express terms

Time of performance

'Time is of the essence' clause – though express stipulations as to time are treated as conditions in commercial contracts *[Bunge Corporation v Tradax, 1981]*

Price

Used to allow, stop or limit supplier increasing price through life of contract. Eg fixed price clause; contract price adjustment clause

Testing, inspection and acceptance clauses

- Buyer not legally bound to accept delivery of goods before acceptance and/or testing to ascertain conformance
- Buyer has right to reject goods for specified reasons
- Right of inspection clause: outsourcer right of access to inspect supplier operations
- Schedule performance clause: condition of contract that certain tasks be performed according to a defined schedule

Subcontracting

Subcontracting (non-assignment) clause may be used to prevent contractor subcontracting part of contract without prior written consent of buyer.

Risks and insurance

- Stipulating risk management processes: eg use of Risk Register, Warning Procedure and Risk Reduction Meetings (NEC)
- Requiring supplier to have necessary insurances to cover liabilities and indemnities: eg employer's liability; public liability; professional indemnity; product liability

Contract variation

- Requirements for change control procedures and variation in contract terms
- Contract price adjustment (CPA) clause: allowing upward or downward revision of fixed price (linked to actual cost increases or decreases or specified indices)

Claims

Provision for contractors to submit claims (for additional time and/or cost) to compensate for negative effect of specified contingencies ('compensation events') on contract performance. (Intended to limited claims or disputes arising during projects.)

Force majeure clauses

Release parties from liability in circumstances where failure results from circumstances which were unforeseeable, for which they are not responsible and which they could not have avoided or overcome (eg war, terrorism, riot, earthquake, flood, industrial dispute).

Duration and renewal

- Duration period or contract term
- Extension or renewal clause: option to continue under the same contract.

The impact of incoterms

Incoterms (International Commercial Terms):

- Set of contractual terms, designed to be understood and interpreted worldwide.
- No legal requirement to adopt incoterms BUT if incoterm adopted into contract, both parties agree to be bound by detailed specifications laid out in *Incoterms 2010*.
- Incoterms specify obligations of buyer and seller re: where delivery should be made; when risk and responsibility pass from seller to buyer; who insures and at what level; and who raises particular documents.

INCOTERM	NAME	RISK AND RESPONSIBILITY PASS AT:
EXW	Ex works ...	named place
FCA	Free carrier ...	named place
FAS	Free alongside ship ...	named port of shipment
FOB	Free on board ...	named port of shipment
CFR	Cost and freight ...	named port of destination
CIF	Cost, insurance and freight ...	named port of destination
CPT	Carriage paid to ...	named place of destination
CIP	Carriage and insurance paid to ...	named place of destination
DAT	Delivered at terminal ...	named terminal at place of destination
DAP	Delivered at place ...	named place of destination
DDP	Delivered duty paid ...	named place of destination

OWN NOTES

OWN NOTES

CHAPTER 11

Implied Terms: Sale of Goods

Contracts for the sale of goods

Sale of Goods Act 1979

Applies to contracts for the **sale of goods**: seller transfers or agrees to transfer **property** (ownership/title) in goods to buyer for a **money consideration** called the price.

Contracts for **SALE** (commitment to transfer ownership):

Includes: bargain + sale; sale + delivery; agreement to sell (property passes at future time); credit sale and conditional sale
Does not include:
- Hire of goods or hire purchase (possession, not ownership)
- Contracts of exchange or barter (consideration in goods, not money)

Contracts for sale of **GOODS**

Includes:
- 'Chattels personal' (tangible, movable property) *other than* 'things in action' (debts, shares, IP: can only be protected by action at law)
- 'Specific goods' (specifically identified at time of contract) OR 'unascertained goods' (defined generally by description, or unidentified part of specific whole)
Does not include: services and skills (work and materials) *[Stewart v Reavell's, 1952]*

Implied terms in the Sale of Goods Act 1979

The implied term as to title: s12

Seller is deemed to undertake:

- As a **condition**, that he has (or will have when property passes) a right to sell the goods
- As a **warranty**, that the goods are free from any charge or encumbrance not disclosed to the buyer, and that the buyer will enjoy quiet possession of them.

Protection when:

- Seller turns out not to be true owner of goods [Rowland v Divall, 1923]
- Trader buys goods which cannot be marketed due to patent restriction [Niblett v Confectioners' Materials Co, 1921]

The implied term as to description: s13

'Sale by description':

- Contract includes some description of goods and
- Buyer contracts in **reliance** on description [Varley v Whipp, 1900] – even if buyer sees goods [Beale v Taylor, 1967], if not obvious that description is inaccurate.

Implied condition that goods correspond with description [Re Moore & Landauer, 1921]

The implied terms as to satisfactory quality and fitness for purpose: s14

Where seller supplies goods in the course of a business, implied term that:

- Goods supplied are of **satisfactory quality:** state or condition, taking into account description, price and circumstances (eg secondhand, urgently manufactured).
- 'Free from minor defects' (including damage through poor packaging by seller) except for:
  — Defects specifically drawn to buyer's attention before contract and/or
  — Defects which buyer's examination before contract ought to have revealed.
- Goods supplied are **fit for purpose** for which goods of that kind are commonly bought (eg unfit where used in 'normal' ways, and do not work properly; fail after short time; are unsafe).
  — Goods must be fit at time of sale [Grant v Australian Knitting Mills, 1936] and remain fit for reasonable time after sale
  — If buyer is going to use goods for particular (unusual) purpose, must notify seller [Griffiths v Peter Conway Ltd, 1939]
- Where buyer makes known to seller any **particular purpose** for which goods are being bought, goods supplied are reasonably fit for that purpose, except where buyer does not (or it would be unreasonable to) rely on seller's skill or judgement.

The implied term as to sale by sample: s15

'Sale by sample': buyer examines sample of goods to be bought, typical of the bulk, + contract term (express or implied) that sale is by sample.

Implied term that:

- The bulk shall correspond with the sample in quality
- Buyer shall have reasonable opportunity to compare bulk with sample
- Goods shall be free from any defect rendering them unsatisfactory, which would not be apparent on 'reasonable examination' of sample [Godley v Perry, 1960]

If bulk does not correspond with sample, buyer can either reject or retain the whole: cannot accept sample and reject the rest, unless the seller agrees.

Exemption clauses

Parties can expressly agree to oust or vary SGA-implied terms *but* subject to Unfair Contract Terms Act 1977: exclusion and limitation clauses not permitted in consumer contracts and only permitted in other contracts where 'reasonable': fair and reasonable to be included, having regard to circumstances which were, or ought reasonably to have been, known to parties when contract was made.

11

OWN NOTES

CHAPTER 12

Transfer of Property, Risk and Title

Transfer of property

Transfer of property = transfer of ownership (vs possession: physical control of goods)

Timing of transfer important:

- If goods accidentally damaged or destroyed: risk depends on ownership
- If buyer or seller becomes bankrupt: bankrupt's property vests in trustee
- If goods damaged or destroyed by third party: different rights of owner
- In deciding right to sell (*nemo dat* **rule**)
- In deciding whether unpaid seller can sue for price.

Two principles of transfer of property

Property in unascertained goods cannot pass before being **ascertained** (SGA s 16) *[Hayman v McLintock, 1907]*. Goods may be ascertained by seller 'appropriating' stock to buyer: eg setting aside or labelling.

Property in goods passes from seller to buyer at such time as the **parties intend** it to pass (eg when goods paid for): (SGA s17) *[Ward v Bignall, 1968]*. Intention evidenced by: contract terms; conduct; circumstances (eg trade custom)

If parties do not indicate intention as to time of transfer (SGA, s 18):

- **Rule 1**. Unconditional contract for sale of specific goods in deliverable state: property passes at time of contract. ('Deliverable state': when buyer would be bound under contract to take delivery. *[Tarling v Baxter, 1827)*
- **Rule 2.** Contract for the sale of specific goods where seller has to do something to put goods into deliverable state: property only passes when this has been done and buyer notified. *[Underwood v Burgh Castle Brick and Cement Syndicate, 1922]*
- **Rule 3.** Contract for sale of specific goods in deliverable state, where seller has to weigh, test or measure to ascertain price: property only passes when this has been done and buyer notified. *[Turley v Bates, 1863]*
- **Rule 4.** Goods delivered on 'approval' or 'sale-or-return' basis: property passes
  (a) When buyer signifies acceptance, or 'adopts transaction' *[Elphick v Barns, 1880]*

12

(b) If buyer retains goods without rejecting them within a fixed or reasonable time [*Poole v Smith's Car Sales, 1962*]

- **Rule 5.** Contract for sale of unascertained goods sold by description: property passes when goods *of that description* and in a **deliverable state are** *unconditionally appropriated* to transaction by one party with *assent* of other [*Carlos Federspeil v Charles Twigg, 1957*]
  - 'Appropriation' usually involves eg despatch or delivery: not unconditional if seller reserves right of disposal until conditions filled (reservation of title clause)
  - 'Assent' (express or implied) may precede appropriation [*Pignataro v Gilroy, 1919*]
  - Unascertained goods forming part of an identifiable bulk: property passes when buyer pays for goods (s20 SGA amended): buyer becomes 'owner in common'.

The passing of risk

General rule

Unless otherwise agreed, **risk passes with property** (SGA, s 20) – *not* with possession.

Before property passes, goods are at seller's risk (even if goods in possession of buyer)

As soon as property has passed, goods are at buyer's risk: buyer liable to pay the agreed price for goods even if lost or damaged (even if still in possession of seller).

Rule may be modified by (a) agreement, (b) trade custom or (c) negligence of possessor/ bailee.

Exceptions to general rule

Passing of property delayed by buyer: buyer bears risk of deterioration during delay

Delivery delayed by fault of either party: party bears risk of consequential loss (s20)

Bailee (holding goods for owner): duty to take reasonable care of goods (s20)

Goods in transit to buyer: seller bears abnormal risks of deterioration in transit (s 33)

Passing of property deferred until goods paid for: goods at buyer's risk after delivery.

Property passes to buyer before delivery: seller has duty of reasonable care pending delivery.

Goods sent by sea: seller must give advance notice of shipment to enable insurance, and notify any changes in risk: if not, goods are at seller's risk (s 32).

Perishing of specific goods

Contract becomes void (and price, if paid, can be recovered) where:

- Specific goods have, unbeknown to parties, perished at time contract was made (SGA s6).

- Specific goods perish *between* time contract made and completion of sale (s7), with no fault on either side.

Contract for the sale of *unascertained* goods, where goods earmarked for fulfilment have perished: seller must obtain and supply other goods of like description and quality.

Transfer of title

'Title' = rightful ownership of goods. General rule: **nemo dat quod non habet** (nobody can give what he does not possess)

Sale of goods by person who does not own them (or have authority or consent of owner): title usually does not pass to buyer (s21).

True owner can recover goods at law without paying any compensation to buyer.

Exceptions to *nemo dat*

Estoppel: owner is by conduct precluded from denying seller's authority to sell (s21) *[Easter Distributors v Goldring, 1957]*

Sale under voidable title: seller derives title from earlier sale which was voidable: if *not* avoided at time of second sale, buyer acquires good title if buys in good faith (s 23) *[Lewis v Averay, 1972]*

Sale by seller in possession: seller has sold to another buyer, but retained possession of goods or title documents: second purchaser can obtain good title if buys in good faith (s 24) *[Worcester Works Finance v Cooden, 1972]*

Sale by buyer in possession: seller has possession but not yet ownership of goods: purchaser can obtain good title to goods if buys in good faith (s 25).

Sale by a mercantile agent: mercantile sales agent acting within authority binds the principle: purchaser has good title (subject to Factors Act 1889)

Sale of a motor vehicle on hire-purchase: first private purchaser to acquire vehicle in good faith will acquire good title.

Sale under special powers: eg sale by court order.

Delivery and acceptance

Seller's duty to deliver

Seller has duty to deliver, and buyer duty to accept and pay for, goods subject to a contract of sale, in accordance with its terms: s27.

Unless seller agrees, payment and delivery are concurrent obligations (s 28)

Place of delivery: if not expressly stated, seller's place of business (s 29)

Time of delivery: if not expressly stated, 'within a reasonable time' (s 29). Specific time may **be stated (or reinstated, if waived:** *Charles Rickards v Oppenheim, 1950)* as condition.

Expense needed to put goods into deliverable state: borne by the seller (s 29)

Delivery of wrong quantity

Less than contracted: buyer may reject – but if accepts, must pay contract rate.

More than contracted, buyer may reject excess *or* accept (and pay for) whole.

Additional goods of different description: buyer can reject whole or accept contracted and reject non-contracted goods (s30).

Delivery by instalments

Contract makes no provision for instalments: buyer *not bound* to accept (s 31)

Contract provides for instalment delivery, single payment: if any instalment is defective, buyer may repudiate the contract (s 35)

Contract provides for instalment delivery and payment: breaches may be treated as severable (eg buyer failure to pay one instalment: *Maple Flock v Universal Furniture Poducts, 1934]*, or as repudiation of entire contract *[Munro v Meyer, 1934]*, depending on severity.

Buyer's duty to accept

The buyer is deemed to have accepted goods (s35) when:

- Buyer signals acceptance to seller (eg authorised signature on delivery note)
- Buyer performs any act in regard to delivered goods implying ownership (eg re-selling)
- Buyer retains goods after lapse of reasonable time, without signalling rejection *[Bernstein v Pamsons Motors, 1987]*

OWN NOTES

OWN NOTES

CHAPTER 13

Remedies for Breach in Sale of Goods Contracts

Remedies of the seller

'Unpaid seller' (SGA s 38) when whole price has not been paid or tendered *or* eg a bill of exchange or cheque has been dishonoured s38(1).

Statutory remedies (SGA) + remedies in contract (eg 'reservation of title' clause).

Statutory remedies of unpaid seller against the goods
- **Lien** (ss 41–43): right of unpaid seller in possession of goods (for which property has passed to buyer) to *retain them* (refuse delivery) until price paid or debt secured/satisfied.
  - Operates until seller paid; credit term expires; or buyer becomes insolvent (s 41).
  - Only enforceable against goods in respect of which price is owing
  - Lost: when goods delivered to carrier without right of disposal reserved; when buyer or agent lawfully obtains possession; by waiver (s 43)
- **Stoppage in transit** (ss 45–46): seller stops carrier delivering goods to insolvent buyer (to whom property in the goods has passed), in order to preserve right of lien.
  - Take possession, or give notice to carrier in possession, before transit complete
- **Right of resale** (s 48). Exercise of lien or stoppage-in-transit confers right to resell if:
  - Goods are perishable
  - Seller gives notice of intention and buyer does not tender price in reasonable time
  - Right of resale reserved in contract

Statutory remedies of unpaid seller against the buyer
- **Action for the price** (s 49). Seller may sue buyer for price where:
  - Property has passed to buyer and buyer fails to pay price as contracted;
  - Price unpaid on date specified in contract (whether or not goods delivered, property passed to buyer or goods appropriated to contract).
- **Action for damages for non-acceptance** (s 50). If buyer wrongfully neglects or refuses to accept and pay for goods, and property not passed, seller can sue for damages.
  - Where available market for goods, damages = difference between contract price and market price at time of acceptance or refusal to accept (s 50).

13

Goods sold under retention of title

Retention of title (Romalpa) clause: express stipulation by seller that property will not pass to buyer until seller has been paid in full *[Aluminium Industrie Vaassen BV v Romalpa Aluminium Ltd, 1976]*.

Gives unpaid seller right to repossess goods (eg from insolvent buyer) *if:*

- Goods are still in the possession of buyer
- Goods are identifiable (ie not mixed with other goods)
- Goods are in their original state (ie not subjected to any manufacturing process).

Remedies of the buyer

Statutory remedies (SGA ss 51–54)

Right of repudiation (rejection and non-payment)

Damages for non-delivery (s 51). Buyer can purchase substitutes at market price: damages = amount by which market price (when delivery due) exceeds contract price.

Order of court for specific performance, in contract for specific or ascertained goods (s 52)

Damages for breach of warranty: buyer may set off breach in reduction of price, or claim damages (s 52). Damages = difference in value between goods of contracted quality and goods actually delivered *or* cost of remedying defect by putting goods into sound condition.

Special damages for additional loss (s 53) – eg loss of profits on re-sale.

OWN NOTES

13

OWN NOTES

CHAPTER 14

Implied Terms: Supply of Goods and Services

Contracts not covered by the Sale of Goods Act 1979

Contracts of hire (bailment of goods only: ownership does not pass) – covered by Supply of Goods and Services Act 1982 (SGSA)

Contracts of hire purchase (bailment of goods + option to purchase) – covered by Supply of Goods (Implied Terms) Act 1973

Contracts for work and materials (substance of contract is buying of skill: *Robinson v Graves, 1935*) – covered by SGSA

Contracts of exchange (consideration in goods, not money) – governed by SGSA

The Supply of Goods and Services Act 1982

Contracts for the transfer of goods *(works and materials, exchange)*

Section 2: implied term on title (similar to SGA s12)

Section 3: implied terms on transfer by description (SGA s13) and sample (SGA s15)

Section 4: implied term on satisfactory quality and fitness for purpose (SGA s14)

Contracts for the hire of goods

Section 7: implied term on title: owner has right to transfer *possession* of goods to bailee.

Section 8: implied term on hire by description

Section 9: implied term on satisfactory quality and fitness for purpose

Section 10: implied term on hire by sample

Contracts for the supply of services

'Contracts for the supply of a service' where the supplier is acting in the course of business – *NOT* contracts of employment, apprenticeship, services of advocate in a court or tribunal or company director to firm.

14

Section 13: implied term that supplier will carry out the service with **reasonable care and skill** *[Greaves & Co v Baynham Meikle & Partners, 1975]*

Section 14: implied term that, where time of service not fixed by contract, supplier will carry out service within a **reasonable time.**

Section 15: implied term that, where consideration not determined by contract, party contracting with supplier will pay a **reasonable charge** *(quantum meruit).*

Exclusion of implied terms

Section 16: exclusion or limitation of liability for **breach** of implied terms is subject to s11 UCTA 1977.

NB: s13 specifically imposes liability for **negligence**: liability cannot be excluded for death or personal injury; for other losses, can only be excluded if 'reasonable'.

OWN NOTES

OWN NOTES

CHAPTER 15

Agency and Bailment

Creation of agency

Nature of agency

Agency is a relationship which arises when one person (agent: A) is authorised to act as representative of another (principal: P), and to effect P's legal rights and obligations.

A is the instrument for entering into legal relations between P and a third party (T).

As long as A acts within delegated authority, P bound by transactions made by A with T.

When A enters into contract on behalf of P, contract is between P and T: A need not have capacity to contract, generally has no rights or liabilities in contract.

Formation of agency

By express agreement: P appoints A to act for him. (Not necessarily a contract eg if no consideration is paid to the agent.)

By implied agreement: P places A in a position in which it would customarily be accepted that A would have authority to act for P: mutual consent implied by conduct.

By ratification: P ratifies or adopts a contract entered into by A purporting to act as P's agent (even if no agency exists or beyond the scope of A's authority): contract becomes binding on P and T. Only valid where:

- A purports to act as agent and clearly identifies P *[Keighley, Maxted v Durant, 1901]*
- P exists and is competent to contract when contract made *[Kelner v Baxter, 1866]*
- P has full knowledge of A's actions or is willing to adopt them, at ratification
- P is willing to ratify the whole contract
- P ratifies before time fixed for performance or within a reasonable time
- P signifies his intention to ratify (by affirmation or conduct)
- The contract itself is not illegal or void.

By estoppel: P is 'estopped' (prevented) from denying that A has authority to make contracts on his behalf, having (by word or conduct) made representation ('holding out') to others that A has this authority. A has 'apparent or ostensible' authority where:

- One person allows another, not his agent, to *appear* **as his agent** *[Freeman and Lockyer v Buckhurst Park Properties, 1964]*

15

- P fails to notify T (who has dealt with A) that A's authority is terminated
- P 'holds A out' as having more authority than he actually has by agreement.

By necessity: A is entrusted with another's property and an emergency arises requiring action to preserve it. A has 'implied authority' *[GN Railway v Swaffield, 1874]* where:

- P's property is entrusted to A (eg perishable goods entrusted to carrier)
- Emergency makes it necessary for A to act
- A is unable to communicate with P to obtain instructions
- A's action was in good faith in P's interests.

Types of agent

General agent: authority to act in ordinary course of trade or profession eg: factor; broker; commercial agent; *del credere* agent; banker; company directors and officers; partner in partnership

Special agent: authority limited to a particular act, not in ordinary course of trade

The authority of an agent

Actual authority (authority P has agreed A shall have) v **apparent authority** (A's authority as it appears to others, as held out by P *[Watteau v Fenwick, 1891]*)

If A acts **without authority**: alleged P not bound; T not bound; A liable to T for breach of warranty of authority

If A acts **in excess of actual authority**: P bound (if A acted within apparent authority) but A may be liable to P for breach of their agreement.

Liability to third parties

A **discloses** to T that he is acting as agent for P: contract between P and T. A has no rights or liabilities – *unless:* A expressly accepts personal liability; A is liable by custom of trade; A purports to act for non-existent P; A refuses to disclose P's identity when required; A purports to act on behalf of company not yet incorporated.

A enters contract appearing to be the principal (**P undisclosed**).

- T on discovering true position may hold A *or* P bound (not both).
- Undisclosed P may intervene and claim against T, if A had authority to act for P when made contract; terms consistent with agency *[Humble v Hunter, 1948];* and T cannot show that he wanted to deal with A and no-one else.

The relationship between principal and agent

Where there is no contract, or contract terms unclear, rights and duties of A and P will be implied by the **common law**.

Duties of A to P

A must perform agency by obeying P's lawful instructions *[Turpin v Bilton, 1843]*

A must perform agency with reasonable care and skill *[Chaudry v Prabhakar]*

A must render an account when required (monetary and factual)

A must act personally, except where delegation authorised, customary or necessary.

Uberrimae fidei: A must not act in own benefit; or breach confidentiality.

Breach of duty = breach of agency agreement: P may sue A for damages for loss, or to recover benefit; P may sue T where T is party to fraudulent breach (eg bribe)

Duties of P to A

P must indemnify A for expense and liability arising from proper performance of duty (*excluding* liability from A's negligence, breach of duty, insolvency *[Duncan v Hill, 1873]*).

P must pay A remuneration, where agreed *[Re Richmond Gate Property, 1965]*

The Commercial Agents (Council Directive) Regulations 1993

Apply specifically to 'commercial agents' (self-employed intermediaries), re: agency contract; commission payable; periods of notice; compensation for termination.

Termination of agency

By complete performance (completion of transaction or expiration of fixed period)

15

By unilateral revocation (by P) or **renunciation** (by A) – unless the agency is *'irrevocable'* (A's authority is coupled with an interest to be protected, or A has started to perform duties and incurred liabilities).

By operation of law: eg death, insanity or bankruptcy of A or P; frustration.

Termination of agency ends actual authority, but A may still have apparent authority – and P will still be bound (except for termination by death or bankruptcy of P).

Bailment

Bailment occurs where a person has custody (not ownership) of another's assets eg:

- Seller who retains goods when property has passed to buyer
- Buyer who takes delivery of goods while seller retains property
- Buyer who takes delivery but then rejects goods
- Seller from whom buyer has agreed to collect goods but fails to do so
- One party 'lent' items by another (eg designs or special tools)
- Contract of bailment (eg leaving items for servicing)

Bailee:

- Has duty of taking reasonable care of goods
- Is liable if wrongfully fails to return goods to bailor at any time agreed
- Has liability for damage to goods (but may sue third party, holding damages on trust for bailor)
- May not sell goods (unless reasonable notice given, funds held in trust for bailor).

OWN NOTES

OWN NOTES

CHAPTER 16

Assignment and Subcontracting

Privity of contract

Doctrine of privity: contract creates personal obligation; only original contracting parties acquire enforceable rights or liabilities under it *[Dunlop Pneumatic Tyre Co v Selfridge, 1915]*

Restrictive: how to ensure rights of third party are enforceable?

Doctrine now subject to **Contracts (Rights of Third Parties) Act 1999**

- Third party may enforce term if: contract expressly states he may; contract purports to confer a benefit on him; parties intended term to be enforceable.
- Parties may not (unless expressly provided) **vary or cancel** contract without consent of third party, if third party relying on term.
- Promisor not doubly liable to promisee *and* third party in respect of loss.

May join person intended to benefit as party to **a contract under seal (deed).** (Specialty contract does not require consideration.)

Exceptions and limitations to the doctrine of privity

Contracting party is operating on behalf of a group *[Jackson v Horizon Holidays, 1975]*

Collateral contracts or warranties: contract between A and B relates to C eg there is a contract between A and C in which C can sue. *[Shanklin Pier Ltd v Detel Products Ltd, 1951]*

Third party rights in tort of negligence (Chapter 17); indemnities (Chapter 10); liability of agent to third parties (Chapter 15)

Assignment of rights and benefits: person entitled to benefit of a contract may assign (transfer) it to a third party.

Assignment and novation

Subcontracting: B (supplier) enters separate contract with C (subcontractor) under which C will *perform some or all of B's obligations* under main contract between A (buyer) and B, which remains in place and in force.

16

Assignment: B *transfers benefit of main contract* with A to third party C.

Novation: main contract between A and B is *replaced by a new one* between A and C: C steps into B's shoes; B falls out of picture.

Assignment

Voluntary assignment. Person entitled to benefit of a contract may assign (transfer) it to a third party, who is then entitled to sue other party to contract to obtain the benefit.

- Most contractual rights (eg to receive payment of debt) can be assigned, unless otherwise agreed – *except* personal rights; employer's right to employees' service.
- Statutory right to assign (Law of Property Act) if absolute assignment in writing.
- Limited by *nemo dat:* if assignor's title is defective, so is that of assignee.

Assignment by operation of law. Automatic transfer of rights and duties of eg deceased to personal representative *[Beswick v Beswick, 1968];* or bankrupt to trustee in bankruptcy.

Subcontracting

Separate contract in which supplier B agrees with subcontractor C that C will perform some or all of B's obligations under a main contract with buyer A.

Key features of subcontracting:

- Main contract stays in place and in force (unlike novation)
- B generally remains liable to A for performance of the main contract: B is liable to A for default in performance by C
- A is *not* usually entitled to sue C for breach: no direct contract between them.

Contract can generally be subcontracted, provided no express clause prohibiting subcontracting or assignment, in the contract between A and B.

Incorporating terms of the main contract

B will generally want subcontract with C expressly to incorporate key terms of main contract with A, where consistent so that C agrees to carry out work 'based on' main contract terms.

If no express incorporation, main contract terms *not* necessarily implied into subcontract.

B or C may be reluctant to tie subcontract to terms of main contract ('back to backing'), if better terms can be negotiated than main contract.

Common contract clauses for subcontracts

Commencement and duration

- Scope and level of services
- Payment terms
- Liability and indemnities
- Subcontracting and assignment

- Contract variations
- Performance management
- Transfer of service contracts (TUPE obligations)
- Dispute resolution
- Termination: express provisions allowing B to terminate subcontract where: main contract is terminated; subcontractor is in breach of contract; subcontractor becomes insolvent; subcontractor is subject to change of control, management or key personnel.

OWN NOTES

CHAPTER 17

Negligence

General principles of tort

'Tort':

(a) Breach of a *legal* duty or infringement of *legal* right
(b) Arising *independently of contract*, which
(c) Gives rise to a claim for *unliquidated damages* (determined by court).

Liability in tort

In general, liability is based on **fault**. Defendant's conduct must have been: intentional or reckless or negligent (failing to pay attention to consequences as a reasonable person would do) – *except* torts of **strict liability**: liable regardless of intention or negligence.

Defendant's conduct must be an **effective cause** of claimant's loss: **'but for' test** [*McWilliams v Sir William Arrol Ltd, 1962*]

Personal liability of tortfeasor to injured person + **vicarious liability** eg employer's liability for acts of employees 'in course of employment'. (Employer never vicariously liable for torts of independent contractors.)

Defences and remedies in tort

Defences

Consent (*volenti non fit injuria:* 'to one who consents, no injury is done'): claimant was aware of risk of harm and consented to risk. (No defence to strict liability.)

Inevitable accident: could not have been foreseen or avoided by any reasonable precautions. (No defence to strict liability, where fault is immaterial.)

17

Statutory authority: backing of statute to perform act complained of – but requirement to exercise statutory authority *reasonably.*

Contributory negligence: claimant guilty of negligence contributing to cause of injury (leads to reduced damages).

Remedies

Usually, **unliquidated damages** (not predetermined by the parties), based on compensating claimant for loss suffered.

Tort rules on 'remoteness' different from contract rules: see below.

The tort of negligence

Negligence: breach of a legal duty to take care which results in damage. Claimant must prove:

- **Duty of care – 'neighbour' principle**
  - Duty to take reasonable care to avoid act or omission which can be reasonably foreseen as likely to injure 'neighbour' (person likely to be affected by act or omission: NB no contractual relationship)
  - Owed by manufacturer to consumers [Donoghue v Stevenson, 1932]
  - Owed by employer to employees [Wilsons & Clyde Coal v English, 1938]
  - Includes liability for negligent **statements** causing **economic loss** made in circumstances where (a) **special relationship** between parties, (b) reasonable for claimant to rely on statement, (c) party making statement has not expressly disclaimed responsibility. [Hedley Byrne & Co Ltd v Heller & Partners Ltd, 1963]
- **Breach of duty of care**
  Defendant failed to take degree of care 'reasonable man' would take in circumstances.
  - If acts or purports to act in professional capacity, must show care and skill of profession [Bolam v Friern Hospital, 1957] – depending on ordinary standards and practices of the time [Roe v Minister of Health, 1954]
  - Burden of proof rests on claimant – except where facts speak for themselves (res ipsa loquitur): presumption of negligence means that burden of proof shifts to defendant [Scott v London and St Katherine Docks Co, 1865]
- **Resultant loss**
  - Causal link between defendant's conduct and damage incurred.
  - Loss not too remote: 'but for' test [McWilliams v Sir William Arrol Ltd, 1962]
  - Loss not too remote: 'reasonable foreseeability' test [The Wagon Mound, 1961]
  - Pure economic loss (not consequent on physical damage) too remote to be recoverable in tort – except re negligent misstatement. [Spartan Steel and Alloys Ltd v Martin & Co Ltd, 1973; Simaan General Contracting Co v Pilkington Glass Ltd, 1988]
  - Liability of subcontractors

Product liability and defective goods

Civil liability

- **Contract-based**: goods not of satisfactory quality or fit for purpose (SGA 1979)
- **Tort of negligence**: manufacturer's duty of care to consumer *[Donoghue v Stevenson; Andrews v Hopkinson, 1957]*.
  — Fault may arise through: poor production or assembly processes; or inadequate warnings or directions for use.
  — If item is defective, rendering it dangerous, manufacturer liable for injury caused .
  — If item is defective in quality, manufacturer liable in contract only: not liable for third-party economic loss *[Simaan v Pilkington; Murphy v Brentwood DC, 1990]*
- **Consumer Protection Act 1987: Part I (defective goods)**
  — Protects consumers (who otherwise cannot claim for breach of contract *or* negligence, if producer was not negligent: *Abousaid v Mothercare, 2001]*
  — **Strict liability** (can't be excluded or limited) for damage caused by defective product. *Primary liability:* producer; brand; importer. *Secondary liability:* supplier (if fails to identify producer, brand or importer).
  — **'Defect'**: safety not such as people generally are entitled to expect
  — **'Damage'** giving rise to liability: death, personal injury, loss or damage to property – *not* loss/damage to product itself or loss/damage less than £275
  — **Defences**: defect attributable to EC compliance; defendant did not supply product; defendant did not supply in course of business; defect did not exist when supplied; defect attributable to another product; defect could not be discovered using scientific and technical knowledge available at the time.

Criminal liability

Consumer Protection Act 1987: Part II (unsafe goods): general duty to ensure that goods comply with safety requirements: failure to do so = criminal offence.

Food Safety Act 1990: strict liability for provision of unfit food (injurious to health; failing to meet safety requirements; not of required quality; falsely described) = criminal offence, even without guilty intent *(mens rea)*. Defences: fault of some other person; reasonable precautions and due diligence.

17

OWN NOTES

CHAPTER 18

The EU Procurement Directives

The law on tendering

Invitation to treat – not an offer capable of acceptance *[Spencer v Harding, 1870]*

Collateral obligations:

- Party inviting tender: duty to consider all compliant tenders received *[Blackpool & Fylde Aero Club Ltd v Blackpool BC, 1990]*
- Party inviting tender: duty to award contract to lowest bidder, if so stated in ITT.
- Party inviting tender: duty to treat unsuccessful bidders on equal terms *[R v The National Lottery Commission (ex parte Camelot plc)]*
- Bidder: implied obligation not to withdraw offer during specified evaluation period.

Tender for 'standing offer': converted into contracts as orders placed *[Great Northern Railway v Witham, 1873]*

The EU procurement directives

Purposes: open up the choice of suppliers; non-discriminatory and competitive markets; free movement of goods and services within EU; VFM public sector purchasing decisions.

Sectors affected

Public Contracts Regulations: all public bodies, including: central government authorities; local government authorities and dependent bodies

- *excluding* contracts covered by 'special sectors' directive; contracts pursuant to international agreements; particular contract types (eg employment contracts, acquisition of existing buildings, financial services)

Public Utilities Regulations: public procurements in the water, energy, transport and postal services sectors

- *exempting* utility activity which is subject to 'effective competition' in the sector.

18

Thresholds and aggregation

Public Contracts:

- Supply and service contracts (central government): 130,000 euros
- Supply and service contracts (other authorities): 200,000 euros
- Works contracts: 5 million euros.

Utilities:

- Supply and service contracts: 400,000 euros
- Works contracts: 5 million euros

Thresholds apply to the total (aggregated) value:

- Contracting authority cannot enter into separate contracts (dis-aggregating demand) with the intention of contract valuations coming in under the thresholds
- Multiple contracts for same type of services, *aggregate value* exceeding threshold: *individual* contracts have to be advertised and awarded under the Regulations.

Remedies in the public and utilities sectors

Suspension of an incomplete contract award procedure

Setting aside of a decision in a completed contract award procedure

An award of damages (in cases where a contract has already been entered)

Contract 'ineffectiveness' (Public Contracts (Amendment) Regulations, 2009) and civil financial penalty (fine)

Procedures for competition

Advertising	• Advertising in OJEU to secure publicity across EU.
Contract award procedures	• Open procedure: no requirement for pre-qualification of suppliers. Tenders must be issued within six days of request by a prospective bidder. Suppliers have 52 days (minimum) to submit bids. *Advantage*: maximum competition. Disadvantage: lack of pre-qualification. • Restricted procedure: suppliers may be pre-qualified, but there must be a pre-stated range of suppliers (5–20) to whom invitations will be sent. Prospective bidders have 37 days (minimum) to register interest and submit the required information for pre-qualification. *Advantage*: ability to pre-qaulify • Negotiated procedure: with advertisement or without (eg in the case of urgency, exclusivity agreements, or no tenders being received under other procedures). Prospective bidders have 37 days (minimum) to register their interest to negotiate. A minimum of three parties must be selected to negotiate. *Disadvantage*: restriction of competition/best value: 'extreme caution' • Competitive dialogue (for large, complex contracts): a process conducted in successive stages to identify potential solutions and gradually reduce the number of tenders to be negotiated. *Advantage*: easier to justify than negotiation; complex solutions developed; phased de-selection. *Disadvantage*: relatively new, complex, uncertain: may deter participation
Other provisions	Contracting authorities may use: • Framework agreements (agreeing terms governing 'standing' contracts for defined periods of up to four years) • Electronic purchasing and tendering/auction systems: completely computerised systems for submission, evaluation and contract award.

The impact of e-tendering

Contracting authorities may use electronic tendering and auction systems which guarantee:

- Precise determination of the exact time and data of receipt of submissions
- No access to data before time limits
- Simultaneous 'opening' of tenders
- Control over the confidentiality of all data.

If e-tendering is used, there are implications for the time scales set for tender stages.

Contracting authorities which decide to hold an electronic auction must state that fact in the contract notice, specifying all details of auction mechanism.

18

Selection and award criteria

Pre-qualification criteria	Buyer may exclude bidders if they fail to meet certain defined criteria in regard to suitability, financial standing and technical competence
Award criteria	• Contracts should be let on the basis of objective award criteria • Buyers generally obliged to award contracts on the basis of lowest price OR most economically advantageous tender (MEAT) • If MEAT used, buyers must make this known to tender candidates and explain the criteria used to assess 'economic advantage'. • All tenderers must have reasonable, equal and timely information about criteria and weighting or ranking of non-price criteria (eg sustainability)

Standstill, feedback and award

Contract award	Results of the tender must be notified to the Official Journal of EU
Standstill	10-day 'standstill' period between decision on contract award and execution: Alcatel period [The Alcatel case]
Right to feedback (debrief)	• Unsuccessful bidders have right to de-brief within 48 days of request. The focus should be on weaknesses that led to rejection of bid, as well as strengths. De-brief should not be used to justify award of contract (and confidential information about successful bid should not be disclosed).
Post-tender negotiation	Restrictions on use under open and restricted procedures No post-tender negotiation on price

OWN NOTES

OWN NOTES

CHAPTER 19

Intellectual Property Law

Types of intellectual property rights

Patents

Protection for new invention, made or used in industry, not obvious to a large number of people, and not *excluded* under Patents Act 2004.

Secured by registration with Intellectual Property Office (UK protection) and/or European Patent Office (EU protection): gives right of control over use of invention, commercial exploitation for 20 years.

Invention by employee in course of employment belongs to employer (but employee compensated for outstanding benefit to employer)

Registered and unregistered design rights

'Design': features of shape, pattern or ornament applied to article by industrial process.

Registered design right (5 year protection, extendable to 25 years): registered at IPO.

Unregistered design right (shorter of 10 years from marketing or 15 years from design).

- Final five years, licensable on payment of royalty.
- Does not attach to items which 'must fit/match' some larger item *[British Leyland v Armstrong Patents, 1986]*

Trade marks

'Trade mark': any sign capable of being *represented graphically* and capable of *distinguishing* goods or services of one undertaking from those of others (Trade Marks Act 1994)

Registered trade mark: the Registrar (UK) or OHIM (Community trade mark)

Copyright

Copyright Protection Act 1988: protection to any original literary, dramatic, musical and artistic work (including computer programmes) not previously published.

Automatic right of protection for 70 years from author's death.

19

IP infringement

Patent: make, use, sell or import something protected by a patent, without permission.

Design: use, sell or import something identical or similar to design, without permission.

Trade mark: use same or similar mark on goods which are same or similar to those covered by registered mark. Where used on *dissimilar* goods, must be likelihood of confusion [*Baywatch Production Co Ltd v The Home Video Channel, 1997*]

Copyright infringement: copying or adaptation of protected works, without permission – *except* where limited use is allowed, with acknowledgement.

Civil infringements. Remedies: injunction + damages or account of profits

The law of passing off

'Passing off': action of a person or organisation that deceives the public by deliberately causing confusion with another (usually much better known) person or organisation.

- Use of similar wrappings or identifications [*Reckitt and Colman v Borden, 1990*] – but trader entitled to use own name [*Wright, Layman & Umney Ltd v Wright, 1949*]
- With element of deception [*Hodgkinson & Corby v Wards Mobility Services, 1994*]
- Where it can be shown that the goods are known to the public, and the public are concerned with their trade origin.

Remedies: injunction [*World Wildlife Fund v World Wrestling Association, 2002*] + damages or account of profits + order to obliterate offending mark.

Intellectual property crime

Criminal IP offences are known as 'Intellectual Property Crime':

- **Counterfeiting**: 'manufacture, importation, distribution, sale of products which falsely carry trade mark of genuine brand without permission and for gain/loss to another'
- **Piracy:** copying, distribution and importation of copyright-infringing works – whether or not direct profit accrues to the seller.

Risks for business: legal liability, security (eg viruses), reputational damage, costs and losses.

Protection of confidentiality and trade secrets

Information confidential if not public knowledge [*Saltman Engineering Co Ltd v Campbell Engineering Co Ltd, 1963*]; of some gravity. Eg commercial records, trade secrets, ideas [*Ackroyds (London) Ltd v Islington Plastics Ltd, 1962*]

Claim for breach re prototypes/idea [*De Maudsley v Palumbo and others, 1996*]: idea must contain significant originality; be clearly identifiable as claimant's idea; be of potential commercial attractiveness; be capable of realisation.

Employer may rely on employee's duty of faithful service to protect trade secrets *[Robb v Green, 1895]* if shows that information was confidential *[Thomas Marshall v Guinle, 1978; Faccenda Chicken v Fowler, 1986]* and that actual or threatened disclosure occurred.

Remedies for breach of confidential information: damages for resulting loss + injunction (exception in non-deliberate use of confidential information: *Seager v Copydex, 1967]*

Confidentiality/non-disclosure clauses

Protection where party needs to give other party access to information about operations, in the course of the contract. Define 'confidential information' + provide for all proper steps to keep confidential.

Where stricter confidentiality required, separate 'non-disclosure agreement' (NDA): conditions under which party may disclose information or ideas in confidence.

Contractual provisions for intellectual property

Background IP: IP which parties bring to contract. Neither party generally gives other extensive rights to background IP: limited use to implement contract.

Foreground IP: new IP created as parties work together: improvements to base product design; customisation or adaptation; 'bespoke' products. Need to negotiate ownership and rights.

Intellectual property rights clauses
- Define what is meant by 'intellectual property rights'
- Establish where ownership of IP is to lie
- Grant other party licences to use IP as required
- Indemnify against infringements.

OWN NOTES

CHAPTER 20

Employment Law

Transfer of undertakings

TUPE 2006 preserves employees' rights to employment protection, terms and conditions on: (a) business transfer or (b) service provision change.

Relevant transfers: eg merger, sale of business, change of licensee, contracting out of services, changing contractors, in-sourcing – within the UK.

Responsibilities of employers and purchasers

All employees employed at transfer automatically become employees of new employer, on the same terms and conditions.

Employees may not be dismissed because of transfer *unless* sound ETO reasons (redundancy).

New employers take over all rights and obligations arising from employment contracts (except some provisions for old age and invalidity).

Some freedom to vary contracts of employment for reasons unconnected with transfer or sound ETO reasons entailing changes in workforce.

Representatives of affected workers entitled to information and consultation.

Transferor must provide transferee with 'employee liability information'.

Redundancy and dismissal

Dismissal

Termination of employee's contract by employer, with or without notice, including the ending of a fixed-term contract without renewal on the same terms.

Dismissal deemed fair, where: ETO reasons; lack of capability (given training, warnings); misconduct (given warnings); redundancy (given fair selection); legal impediment; other 'substantial' reason.

Dismissal deemed unfair where related to: unfair selection for redundancy; trade union activity; transfer of undertaking; pregnancy; action re statutory rights; lawful industrial action; whistleblowing.

20

To claim unfair dismissal, employee must show (a) qualifying employee (b) dismissed. Employer must then justify reasonableness of dismissal.

Remedies for unfair dismissal: reinstatement; re-engagement; compensation.

Constructive dismissal

Employee terminates employment in response to breach of contract by employer.

Redundancy

Defined (ERA 1996, TURER 1993) as dismissal: where employer has ceased to carry on the business or ceased to carry on business in location; where business requirements for work have ceased or diminished; or for reasons 'not related to individual concerned'.

Selection for redundancy must be undertaken in a fair, reasonable and consistent manner, on objective criteria. Automatically unfair where by: pregnancy or maternity; trade union activity; protected shop workers; trustees of occupational pension scheme.

Entitlement to compensation: statutory + contractual redundancy pay – *unless* of pension age or over, or if 'suitable' offer of alternative employment 'unreasonably' rejected *[Taylor v Kent CC, 1969]*

Duty to consult representatives of recognised trade union (TULRA 1992): must begin 'at earliest opportunity' (minimum 90 days before first dismissal of 100 or more employees)

Duty to notify Secretary of State if 10 or more employees affected.

Discrimination in the workplace

Equality Act 2010

Protected characteristics: age, disability, gender reassignment, marriage and civil partnership, pregnancy and maternity, race, religion or belief, sex and sexual orientation.

Five forms of unlawful discrimination

Direct discrimination: job applicant, employee or former employee is treated less favourably than another because of a protected characteristic.

Indirect discrimination: employer does something which has worse impact on people with protected characteristic than on others – *unless* objectively justified.

Victimisation: person is treated badly because they have complained about discrimination, or done anything to uphold equality law rights.

Harassment: unwanted conduct which violates a person's dignity, or creates an intimidating, hostile, degrading, humiliating or offensive environment.

Discrimination arising from disability: employer treats a disabled person unfavourably because of something connected to their disability, *unless* treatment objectively justified *or* disability unknown.

Legitimate **exceptions**: genuine occupational requirement; legal impediment; national security; religious conviction; specific needs.

Legislation does *not* permit **positive discrimination**: actions which give preference to people with protected characteristics, regardless of genuine suitability or qualification. However voluntary positive action and favourable treatment for disabled people are encouraged.

Specific provisions

Specific provisions exist in regard to: recruitment and selection; working hours, flexible working and time off; pay and benefits; career development (training, promotions and transfers); and management issues (eg dress codes, access to facilities, performance management, discipline, termination).

Remedies for discrimination

Action: informal complaint; formal grievance procedures; claim to Employment Tribunal

Remedies: declaration of discrimination; compensation; recommendation to employer to act within a certain time to remove or reduce bad effects on claimant.

Restraint of trade

Restraint of trade: contract restricts a person wholly or in part from carrying on his trade, business, profession or occupation as he wishes.

Three types of clause in restraint of trade (restrictive covenant): employee leaving employment; vendor of business including goodwill; solus agreement for supply.

General rule: **void at common law**. Enforceable only if 'reasonable':

- Legitimate interest to protect: trade secrets and client connections *[Harris v Littlewoods Organisation, 1978]* – *not* preventing competition or exploiting generally available knowledge *[Faccenda Chicken Ltd v Fowler, 1986]*
- No wider than necessary in area or time *[Mason v Provident Clothing, 1913]*
- Not prejudicial to public interest.

Garden leave clauses: employer pays terminated employee during notice period, but requires him not to attend work. Must be provided for in contract of employment *[William Hill Organisation v Tucker, 1998]*; length no longer than necessary; full salary and benefits paid throughout period.

20

Agency workers

'Agency worker law' regulates individuals' work through employment agencies in the UK.

Traditionally lacking rights of 'employees' *[O'Kelly v Trusthouse Forte plc]*

Agency Workers Regulations 2010: on completion of a qualifying period (12 weeks), agency workers should be no less favourably treated than full-time 'direct' workers performing comparable work with similar level of qualification or skills, in regard to: pay, working time, access to collective facilities and amenities, and access to vacant posts.

Conduct of Employment Agencies and Employment Business Regulations 2003: restrict agencies from abusive practices eg charging workers fees for work.

Gangmasters (Licensing) Act 2004: protection for vulnerable workers in agricultural, shellfish and food packing sectors.

Ethical employment in the supply chain

Codes for minimum acceptable standards usually based on the 'conventions' developed by **International Labour Organisation (ILO):** Eg Declaration on Fundamental Principles and Rights at Work.

Social Accountability 8000 standard covers issues including: child labour; forced and compulsory labour; health and safety; freedom of association and collective bargaining; discrimination; disciplinary practices; working hours; remuneration and management systems.

OWN NOTES

OWN NOTES

CHAPTER 21

The Law on Competition, Bribery and Corruption

UK competition law

Competition Act 1998 outlaws agreements, business practices and conduct which have a damaging effect on competition in the UK.

Chapter 1 Prohibition: agreements, decisions and concerted practices which prevent, restrict or distort competition, or are intended to.

- Eg price fixing; limiting or controlling markets; sharing markets or supply sources; applying different trading conditions to equivalent transactions; making contracts subject to unrelated conditions – with a significant effect on competition.
- Exemptions: individual, block or parallel (covered by EC exemptions).

Chapter 2 Prohibition: abuse by one or more undertakings of a dominant market position.

- Eg: imposing unfair prices; limiting markets to prejudice of consumers; distorting competition; attaching unrelated conditions to contracts.

Monopolies and mergers

'Monopoly': company or cartel supplies or purchases 25% + of all goods or services of a particular type in the UK or region of UK *[South Yorkshire Transport Ltd v MMC, 1993]*

Fair Trading Act 1973: gives OFT powers to regulate:

- Monopolies: may seek assurances of altered business practices *or* refer to Competition Commission.
- Mergers: if turnover exceeds defined amount (Enterprise Act 2002) or merger likely to result in monopoly situation. OFT may refer to Competition Commission.

Merger comes under EC Merger Control Regulation if aggregate worldwide turnover exceeds defined threshold, and at least two parties have EU turnover in excess of a defined threshold. Referred to European Commission.

EU Articles on anti-competitive practices

Article 81: anti-competitive (restrictive) agreements affecting trade between member states *[Hugin Kassregister v Commission, 1979]*

Article 82: abuse of monopoly position affecting trade between member states. Defines monopoly position in terms of **relevant economic strength** *[United Brands v Commission, 1978]*

Article 87: prohibition of State aid by member states which (a) confers economic advantage (b) favouring certain undertakings or sectors.

- Compensation for costs of providing public service does not constitute economic advantage *[Altmark Ruling, 2003]*
- Measures favouring the economy in general do not favour particular undertakings.
- All new or altered State aid has to be notified to the Commission. 'Unlawful aid', not cleared by the Commission, is subject to recovery.

Enforcement of competition law

Competition Act 1998:

- Director General may order company in breach of prohibition to terminate or amend the offending agreement or cease the offending conduct.
- Undertakings in breach (of a certain size) may be liable to a financial penalty of up to 10% of UK turnover.
- Third parties harmed as a result of unlawful practice may claim for damages.
- Cases eg: *Hasbro UK Ltd/Argos Ltd/Littlewoods Ltd, 2003;* 'duplicate kit cartel'

Competition Commission: investigates breaches, hears appeals vs OFT decisions.

Enterprise Act 2002: penalties for individuals operating 'hardcore cartels'; allows consumer bodies to bring 'supercomplaints' about markets to the OFT.

Sector inquiries: market studies by OFT leading to market investigation by CC. Eg: supply of airport services by BAA; groceries retailing market; construction industry.

Sectoral codes of practice: by statutory order (eg Groceries Supply Code of Practice) or voluntary measures (eg Construction Industry Competition Law Code of Conduct)

Bribery and corruption

'Corruption': 'the abuse of public office for private gain' (World Bank) – eg accepting, soliciting or extorting a bribe or inducement; patronage and nepotism; theft of assets.

Problematic cases of gifts and hospitality (especially in some cultures), dealt with in CIPS Code of Ethics re value of gifts; transparency and disclosure.

Bribery Act 2020 creates crimes of:

- **Bribery:** when a person offers, gives or promises to give a 'financial or other advantage' to another individual, in exchange for 'improperly' performing a relevant function (expectation of good faith or impartiality breached)
- **Being bribed:** requesting, accepting or agreeing to accept such an advantage, in exchange for improperly performing such a function or activity.
- **Bribery of foreign public officials**: promising, offering or giving a financial or other advantage: to a foreign public official, directly or through a third party, where such advantage is not legitimately due.
- **Failure of a commercial organisation to prevent bribery on its behalf** (by employee, agent, subsidiary or third party).

Penalties: imprisonment, unlimited fines, confiscation of property; disqualification of directors.

Money laundering

Proceeds of Crime Act 2002, Money Laundering Regulations 2007: offence to obtain, conceal or invest funds or property, if you know or suspect that they are 'criminal property': proceeds of criminal conduct (including tax evasion, bribery and corruption) or terrorist funding.

All businesses required to adopt measures to identify and prevent money laundering and terrorist financing, including: due diligence, disclosing knowledge or suspicion, not 'tipping off' subjects of investigation.

OWN NOTES